Bannockburn for Beginners

Bannockburn for Beginners

RENNIE McOWAN

Rowan Tree Publishing

First published in 2014 by
ROWAN TREE PUBLISHING
Lochbank House, Castle Douglas DG7 1TH

Copyright © Rennie McOwan 2014

ISBN 978-0-9562307-9-9

All rights reserved. No part of this publication may be reproduced or transmitted in any form or by any means, electronic or mechanical, including photocopy, recording, or information storage and retrieval system, without permission from the publisher. This book is sold subject to the condition that it shall not, by way of trade or otherwise, be lent, re-sold, hired out or circulated without the publisher's prior consent.

British Library Cataloguing in Publication Data
A catalogue record for this book is available from the British Library.

Editorial consultant: Patricia Burgess
Cover and design: Annette Peppis & Associates
Cover photograph: Leo Blamire
Illustrations: pp.ii, 71 Route66/Shutterstock; pp.viii, 2, 15, 16, 18, 29, 62, 64 Stoker-13/Shutterstock; pp.4, 6 Nebojsa Dikic/Shutterstock; p.20 losw/Shutterstock; pp.25, 30–31 Leo Blamire; p.35 Cattallina/Shutterstock; pp.36, 38 Piratka/Shutterstock; pp.48, 61 Theo Malings/Shutterstock; pp.52, 54 Naddya/Shutterstock.

Printed and bound in Scotland

DEDICATION

For
TOM AND RICHARD

NOTE FOR READERS

Questions and Things to Do are features of this book. They offer younger readers the opportunity to think about what they have read, and then to work on individual or shared projects.

CONTENTS

Introduction	Remaining Independent	1
Chapter 1	Who's Who	5
Chapter 2	For Scotland's Freedom	17
Chapter 3	Victory at Bannockburn	37
Chapter 4	After the Battle	53
Chapter 5	Remembering Bannockburn	63

the years there was much st
in 1307, before it was compl
ard II, who continued the i
most important battle in Sc

Remaining Independent

In 1286, King Alexander III of Scotland died. He had ruled for nearly 40 years and made peace with England, but all his children had died before him. His three-year-old granddaughter Margaret, known as the 'Maid of Norway', was therefore named his heir. Sadly, she died while travelling to Scotland from Norway.

These events resulted in a crisis over the future of Scotland. As there was now no clear heir to the throne, thirteen rivals claimed the right to be king. When they could not agree amongst themselves, the Scots turned to Edward I of England for arbitration. At his suggestion, John Balliol, Lord of Galloway, was crowned King of Scotland in 1292. He worked hard to restore law and order in the kingdom, and even signed an alliance treaty with France, England's enemy, in 1295.

Edward was angered by this, believing that Balliol should obey him rather than being a ruler in his own right. So in 1296 Edward I invaded Scotland and started what became known as the First War of Scottish Independence. Balliol was captured and sent to England as a prisoner. Edward I then proclaimed himself King of Scotland.

Some Scottish nobles who had lands and family in England swore allegiance to Edward. Many others, though, refused to accept English rule. As a result, a period of Scots resistance followed, led notably by Sir William Wallace. Wallace was eventually captured and executed. A powerful figure then took up the fight to repel the English presence. Robert Bruce, an influential noble who had royal blood, was crowned King of the Scots in 1306.

A year later Edward II inherited the English throne, determined to control Scotland. King Robert fought back and led the Scots in a guerrilla war over the next seven years. This was the war that would climax in 1314 with the most important battle in Scotland's history.

This is the story of the Battle of Bannockburn.

...ert actually had very little t...
...for independence. He was n...
...urs. But that didn't matter. ...
...elt Scotland should be a na...

CHAPTER 1

Who's Who

The struggle for Scottish independence went on over many years. Before the Battle of Bannockburn, English kings regarded the country of Scotland as a part of England.

The coronation of King Robert in 1306 brought a new energy and confidence to the campaign to end English rule in Scotland.

In 1307 King Edward I died and his less experienced son Edward II ascended to the throne of England. He was determined to keep Scotland under English control. The new King Edward saw King Robert as a great threat to his interests in Scotland. Edward feared the Scottish king's popularity. He knew he would have to do something about this man who had been crowned just a year before him.

Unlike King Edward, Robert had neither riches nor honours to offer those who joined him in the fight for Scottish Independence. But that didn't matter. Robert's supporters joined him because they felt Scotland should be a nation of its own. They did not want it to be under the rule of the English king. Edward however felt Scotland was his to rule, just as his father had tried to do.

The two opposing sides were firm in their views. It was just a matter of time before King Edward II, his key nobles and his forces would meet King Robert, his nobles and his independence army in a major encounter. This confrontation would eventually take place close to the strategically important town of Stirling. This fateful meeting would take place at Bannockburn.

This chapter gives an overview of the key figures on both sides who took part in that legendary battle. It describes their backgrounds and allegiances, and reveals what happened to them on those two days in June 1314.

KEY FIGURES

Here is a list of the key people who were involved in the events that led up to the Battle of Bannockburn, or who actually took part in it.

Scotland

King Robert Bruce (1274–1329) was a Scottish nobleman who made claim to the Scottish throne. In 1306 he killed his great rival John Comyn in a fight at Greyfriars monastery in Dumfries. The Church authorities later absolved Bruce of this mortal sin. This event though, did not prevent Robert acceding to the throne and he was crowned king in 1306. He proved to be a great political and military tactician.

Sir Edward Bruce (1276–1318) was the younger brother of Robert Bruce. He could be foolhardy at times, but was a brave soldier. He fought alongside his brother at Bannockburn. He made an unauthorised arrangement with Sir Philip Mowbray, the commander of the garrison at Stirling Castle. This set off the train of events that led to the Battle of Bannockburn.

Sir James Douglas (1286–1330) was also known as the 'Black Douglas' by the English because of the deadly raids he led against them . He was one of the leading Scottish nobles who fought at the battle. It was Sir James who asked King Robert if he could lead the chase for the fleeing King Edward. He nearly caught him, but the English king made it to safety in Dunbar Castle just in time.

Sir Robert Keith (d. 1332) was a leading Scottish knight and general. He was in charge of the Scots cavalry at Bannockburn.

Angus Og, Chief of the Clan Macdonald (c.1270–1330) sheltered Robert Bruce from the English in 1306. In gratitude, King Robert said the clan would always take the special right wing position in the Scottish army. Some sources say the honour was given for support at Falkirk. The clan were on the right at Bannockburn.

Sir Thomas Randolph, Earl of Moray (d. 1332) was the step-nephew of King Robert. He fought for a while on the English side, but rejoined the Scots in the spring of 1314. Sir Thomas famously climbed the Rock of Edinburgh Castle and seized the fortress. At the Battle of Bannockburn he commanded the Scots' vanguard.

Sir Alexander Seton (1290–1332) was a Scottish nobleman who defected from the English side just before the battle. He gave King Robert information that helped him to make key tactical decisions.

England

King Edward I (1239–1307) was known as the 'Hammer of the Scots'. He believed that Scotland should be under English rule. During his long reign he tried to control many parts Scotland. He was never totally successful.

King Edward II (1284–1327) led the English side at the Battle of Bannockburn. He lived in the shadow of his father's strong personality. As a result, some people thought he was a weaker king.

Sir Giles d'Argentan (d. 1314), said to be one of the bravest knights in Europe, was in the group of personal bodyguards to King Edward II. Once Sir Giles had escorted the king to safety, he returned to the battle. There he charged alone towards the Scots and was killed.

Sir Henry de Beaumont, Earl of Buchan (d. 1340) was a Scottish noble who fought for the English. He was also one of those who helped Edward II to escape. As punishment, King Robert stripped him of his earldom.

Sir Henry de Bohun (d. 1314) was an English knight, the nephew of Humphrey de Bohun (below). He was killed on the first day of the battle by Robert Bruce.

Humphrey de Bohun, Earl of Hereford (1276–1322) co-led the English cavalry vanguard on the first day of the battle. Prior to Bannockburn, during King Robert's self created exile, the Earl was given much land and the Castle of Lochmaben that had once belonged to Robert the Bruce.

Sir Robert Clifford (1274–1314) was a senior English soldier. He was present at the Battle of Falkirk, where William Wallace was defeated. Sir Robert died at the Battle of Bannockburn, fighting for Edward II.

Sir Philip Mowbray (d. 1318) was governor of Stirling Castle. Edward Bruce besieged it before the battle, but both sides quickly became deadlocked. Neither could win. Mowbray therefore agreed to Edward's suggestion – that if the English did not relieve the castle by midsummer 1314, he would hand it over to the Scots.

Gilbert St Clare, Earl of Gloucester (1291–1314) led the English vanguard at the Battle of Bannockburn. He was killed at the start of the second day. Afterwards he was regarded as the most high-profile fatality of the battle.

Sir Robert de Umfraville, Earl of Angus (1277–1323) fought at Bannockburn for Edward I. He was taken prisoner after the battle by Robert Bruce, but soon released. However, King Robert stripped him of the ownership of his Scottish lands.

Aymer de Valence, Earl of Pembroke (1275–1324) was appointed Lieutenant of Scotland by Edward II in 1314. He commanded Welsh infantrymen at the battle. He was also one of the knights who helped lead Edward away from the battle in order to avoid capture.

> **DID YOU KNOW?**
>
> The origins of the name Bannockburn (*Allt A' Bhonnaich* in Gaelic) are still not certain. Of course, part of it comes from the burn (stream) that runs through it. But what about 'bannock'? This is a type of scone, and some people say the village might have been a place where bannocks were made. It seems more likely, though, that *bhonnaich* is related to the word for 'blessed', so Bannockburn probably means 'blessed stream'.

WORD LIST

arbitration	=	the process of settling a dispute by listening to all sides
besiege	=	to surround and starve of food and water
cavalry	=	troops mounted on horses
deadlock	=	a position in which neither side can win
patriot	=	a person who vigorously supports his or her country
vanguard	=	an advance party of troops; the first to go into battle

QUESTIONS & THINGS TO DO

- Can you think why 'Bannockburn' might have been named after a holy stream? Look it up in a history book, or check it out online.
- Make a list of the kings and queens of Scotland, together with their dates.
- Choose a clan and draw their tartan.
- Have you heard of any other people in times past who were important in fighting for Scottish independence? See if you can find out their names and what they did.

CHAPTER 2

For Scotland's Freedom

King Robert Bruce was very angry. His brother, Sir Edward, had made a pledge that might ruin everything he had planned and struggled for over many years. Here's what happened.

The King of the Scots had been fighting guerrilla actions against the English armies in Scotland since he was crowned at Scone in Perthshire in March 1306. His reign had not begun well.

His small army had been quickly defeated and scattered. His friends were hanged or fled into hiding. His relatives were imprisoned and cruelly treated. His estates were forfeited.

But still he had continued the fight, determined to succeed in keeping Scotland's independence.

He spent the winter of 1306 in the Western Isles and possibly Ireland. While there, he made plans for overthrowing the invaders in his homeland. He returned to Scotland in 1307 and waged unceasing war against the English. He also fought against the Scots who supported England. Many of these Scottish nobles had lands and interests in both Scotland and England. They were happy to let all of them remain under the authority of the English king.

Robert knew he could not yet win a pitched battle. He did not have enough men or a secure base. But he had outstanding commanders, tested in many a skirmish and ambush. He also made skilful use of the Scottish forests, and of lonely glens and mountains, to hide his small band.

His strategy was clever. He sprang surprise attacks on isolated garrisons of English soldiers, and on the headquarters of their Scottish supporters, and demolished them.

He also defeated sizeable English forces on the ground of his own choosing. For example, he captured strong-points and towns, sacked and burnt the buildings, and destroyed enemy weapons, food and stores. He and his men then melted back into the countryside.

It was the classic guerrilla style of warfare. This is something we have seen often in modern times, during the Second World War and afterwards.

By keeping rigidly to this strategy, he gradually began to drive the English forces back into the main border castles and keeps.

A LESSON IN PERSEVERENCE

A legend sprang up that when Robert Bruce was a fugitive, he took refuge in a cave and watched a spider spinning its web. Every time the web broke, the spider began all over again, persevering until it was completed successfully. It is said that Bruce learnt a valuable lesson from that spider and applied it to his fight against the English. That lesson was: never give up.

Many Scots flocked to join King Robert's standard. He was ruthless with those who didn't. For example, he totally crushed the powerful Comyn family, who did not want him as king.

After overcoming his Scottish opponents, he was free to turn his whole attention to the English forces.

Gradually, the leading Scottish towns and castles fell to him. An exception was Stirling Castle, which was in a strong and dominating position. It controlled all traffic going north and south. It also oversaw east–west activities between Glasgow and Edinburgh. Stirling had an unrivalled strategic importance. It was said to be like a brooch that clasped the Highlands and Lowlands together.

Sir Edward Bruce, King Robert's brother, laid siege to the castle for three months. This eventually forced the castle commander, Sir Philip Mowbray, to enter discussions with him.

The commander said he would surrender if an English army failed to appear within 3 leagues (about 10 miles or 16 kilometres) of the castle by Midsummer's Day 1314.

Edward Bruce impetuously agreed, perhaps carried away by the steady flow of Scottish successes. He had always been a man of action. Indeed, it was he who had encouraged Robert to persevere in the struggle when they had returned to the Scottish mainland after hiding out in the Western Isles.

When King Robert was told about Edward's decision, he was deeply displeased. He knew the pledge meant that the English might now meet the Scots in pitched battle, an event he had deliberately avoided.

Bruce was not sure his men were ready. He knew that the English could put a huge army of armoured knights into the field. He also knew they could produce many archers, who had been very important in helping to win other battles.

It was the archers who had defeated Sir William Wallace at the Battle of Falkirk in 1298. Their hail of arrows broke up the schiltron (ring) of Scottish spearmen. This had opened up gaps and left them prey to the charge of knights on heavy horses.

o o o

Robert Bruce's hit-and-hide tactics had been successful. Now the pattern was to change, and he was uneasy.

But the deed was done, and the pledge had been made.

Stirling Castle had proved a stumbling block for many armies. Now it was to be the prize for the victor of one of the greatest conflicts of the Scottish Wars of Independence.

King Edward II of England was not the iron-hard soldier his father had been. The famous 'Hammer of the Scots' had been a fiercesome opponent, but his son was still determined to accept the challenge from the upstart Scot.

He was certain that if he could defeat the Scots in pitched battle, he could win back everything he had lost in Scotland since Bruce was crowned. After that, he could either rule himself or install a puppet king.

He gathered a huge army of 25,000 foot soldiers armed with spears, axes and swords. He also recruited many Welsh archers armed with longbows.

In addition, he had over 2,000 heavy cavalry. These were expected to crush the Scots troops in the same way that modern tanks can overrun infantrymen.

King Edward also had the help of some Scots, such as the Comyns, MacDougalls and MacNabs, who were fierce opponents of Bruce because of major land and power differences.

It was a vast army for the time, with a supply and baggage train of over 200 wagons. These were full of food, spare arms, equipment and pay for the troops.

King Edward and his commanders were confident of an easy victory. In fact, they were so sure of success that their wagons also carried furniture and other goods to reward nobles once the expected crushing victory had taken place. They even took along a poet, whose task was to celebrate an English victory.

○ ○ ○

Bruce, however, held many cards. His army, although small, was well disciplined and accustomed to command. It was also lean and experienced, and had been together as a close-knit fighting unit for some years.

It was obviously important to prevent the relief of Stirling Castle. But the Scots also had to try to destroy King Edward's army.

Bruce had just two months to bring his army to readiness for a pitched battle.

He had about 7,000 soldiers in all, but only a few hundred light cavalry.

He was determined not to repeat the mistakes of the Battle of Falkirk. He therefore trained his men to quickly form and break the Scottish battle ring, the schiltron (see page 25). He also taught them to counter-attack in formation, a strategy intended to give the men greater mobility than at Falkirk.

As for weaponry, the men were equipped with spears 13 feet (4 metres) long, swords, axes and dirks. They also had protective helmets, chain-mail gloves to hold the spears, and thickly padded coats to stop arrows penetrating their flesh.

THE SCHILTRON

One of the most intimidating sights on the medieval battlefield was a schiltron. This was a tightly packed ring of soldiers standing in concentric circles and holding their very long spears towards the enemy horsemen. In this formation, they looked rather like a spiky hedgehog and were extremely difficult to tackle.

The word 'schiltron' may be German – nobody knows for sure – but it means roughly 'troop shield'. Some schiltrons contained archers in the middle. Whatever the set-up, the entire formation was tightly disciplined and could repel an attack by heavily armed cavalry. King Robert trained his men to operate schiltron formations that could hold their ground, yet also, on command, quickly advance and attack enemy forces. This might involve the men having to 'break hedgehog' and fight in hand-to-hand combat with their other weapons.

A Soldiers with spears, raised at different heights, stand in concentric circles.
B Some schiltrons contained archers in the middle.
C Cavalry could be repelled from all angles thanks to the hedgehog formation.

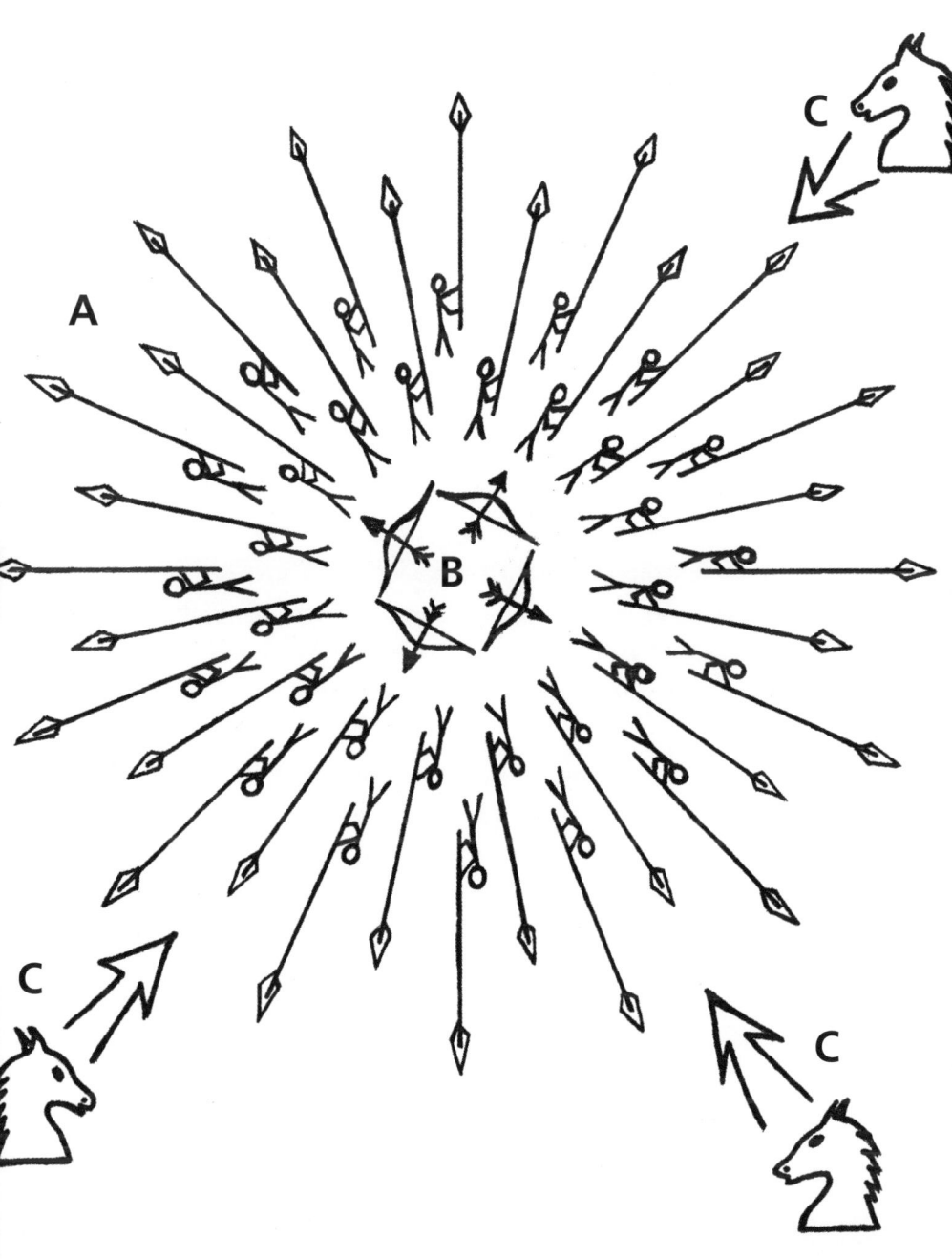

In defence, the schiltron formed an unbroken wall of spears against the charge of the armoured knights. In advance, it relied on numbers to add weight and to press home the attack with levelled spears.

Practice and discipline were essential, and Bruce saw that his men had these in abundance.

He split his force into four divisions under battle-tried commanders. The first was commanded by Thomas Randolph, Earl of Moray, who had captured Edinburgh Castle in a daring raid the year before. The second division was led by Sir Edward Bruce, no doubt worried about what his rash promise to the commander of the castle might bring about. The third was led by the feared Sir James Douglas. And the fourth, the strongest division, was commanded by the king himself.

Next to Bruce, Douglas was the greatest hero among the Scots. Nicknamed 'Black Douglas', he became such a terror to the invaders that mothers used to repeat a rhyme to their children:

> Hush thee, hush thee, do not fret thee,
> The Black Douglas will not get thee!

It was Douglas who had planned the famous recapture of his own castle, Douglasdale in Lanarkshire. When the English garrison had attended church on Palm Sunday, Douglas's men were in the congregation with weapons hidden beneath their cloaks. At his signal – he dropped his cloak and shouted 'A Douglas! A Douglas!' – they fell upon the men from the garrison and killed them all. Then they took the castle, replenished their own stores, and made a great heap of corpses and other unwanted stuff, and set fire to it all. This famous raid was known as the 'Douglas Larder'.

Bruce was also aided by about 2,000 'small folk', the ordinary people who had lost homes and families, and who wanted to join in the fray. They were poorly armed and ill disciplined, but they would go on to play a key part in the battle.

The cavalry, under Sir Robert Keith, were to be kept for a special role.

○ ○ ○

The men in the Scottish army came from nearly all parts of Scotland, including Ross and Moray, Inverness, Elgin and Nairn, Buchan, Mar, Angus, Strathearn, Menteith and Lennox, and from central Scotland and the Borders.

King Robert's own division had Macdonalds from the west, from Kintyre and Argyll, and men from his own area of Carrick, Kyle and Cunningham.

It was a truly national army, with many clans taking part. These included Camerons, Campbells, Frasers, Gordons, Macphersons, Macleans, MacGregors, Mackenzies, Rosses and Sinclairs.

Robert Bruce set up his supply base at Cambuskenneth, in the loop of the River Forth, not far from Stirling.

Meanwhile, on 17th June the English army left its southern bases and marched to Edinburgh. On the 22nd they left the city to make their way to Stirling. They still had two days in which to relieve the castle. It could be clearly seen and drew all eyes to it.

○ ○ ○

To start with Bruce kept his strongest division as a rearguard at the Torwood, between Stirling and Falkirk, with horse patrols keeping

an eye on the enemy. His main troops busied themselves preparing defensive positions covering Stirling.

They made skilful use of the line of the Bannockburn, and of the marshes and bogs that were then plentiful. He ordered pits to be dug, with spikes called calthrops placed inside. These pits were then covered so that the enemy horses and the charging English knights would fall into them and be maimed.

His main position was a good one just inside the line of the New Park, between the Borestone (see page 68) and Bannockburn. His right wing was partly hidden in scrub and forest, while his left wing was along an escarpment, which allowed good observation.

Bruce's plan would force King Edward to attack from the front over difficult ground for horses, or to risk going around the left flank over other difficult terrain.

If King Edward were to attack the left flank, Bruce thought it might present a good opportunity for his own troops to counter-attack. After all, the Scots were familiar with the terrain, but the English soldiers were not.

Later, Bruce withdrew his division from the Torwood into his main position in order to hold the edge of the wood in the New Park. He kept horse patrols out in front.

The men led by Edward Bruce held the high ground to the left. Moray was stationed near St Ninian's Church on the fringe of Stirling to watch the flat ground of the carse. The rest were kept in the Borestone area (near the present-day visitor centre). Tradition has it that the current site of Bruce's statue was his command post during part of the battle.

The ill-disciplined small folk, panting to get at the enemy, were stationed behind Coxet Hill.

The array of Scottish troops must have aroused great anxiety in the defenders of the castle, as they peered from the battlements, watching the sun glint on spears and armour.

BANNOCKBURN FOR BEGINNERS

Key

There continues to be debate as to the exact location of the events on 23 and 24 June 1314. This map is intended to provide a general overview of what may have taken place.

23 June 1314
1 King Robert's division
2 Edward Bruce's division
3 James Douglas's division
4 Thomas Randolph's division
5 Thomas Randolph encounters Robert Clifford
6 Encounter between King Robert and Henry de Bohun

24 June 1314
7 Scottish divisions advance towards the carse
A Disorderly cavalry charge led by the Earl of Gloucester
B English divisions form behind the charging cavalry
X Main battle took place here on 24 June 1314

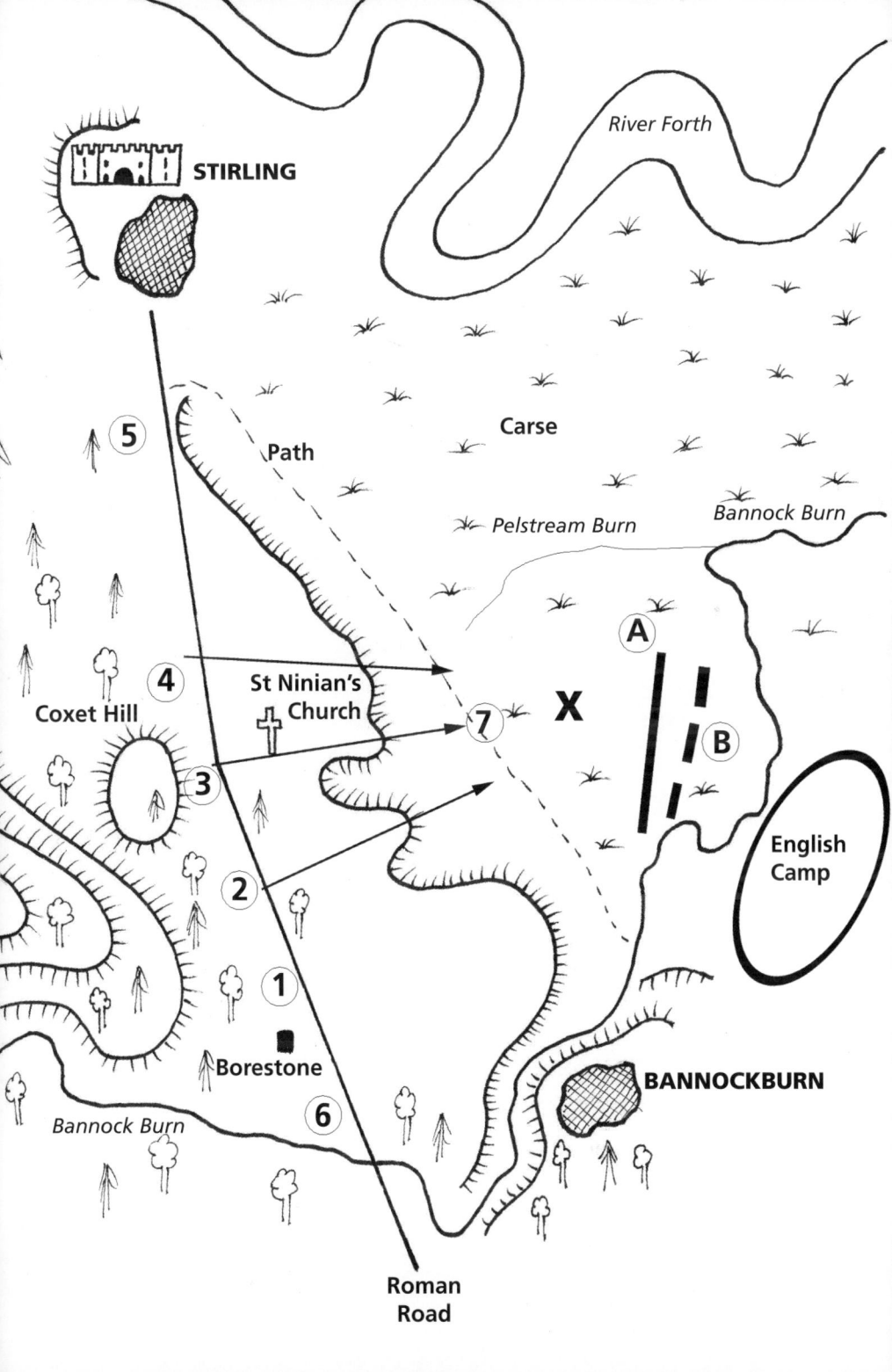

WORD LIST

calthrops	=	spikes placed inside hidden pits; they were designed to maim enemy horses and soldiers
carse	=	a riverside area of flat ground
dirk	=	dagger
escarpment	=	a steep ridge of rock
flank	=	side
garrison	=	a secure building in which troops are based
guerrilla warfare	=	encounters consisting of quick surprise attacks
heavy cavalry	=	armoured men on armoured horses
hedgehog	=	the nickname for a schiltron (see opposite); when the men and spears were in formation, they had a spiky appearance like a hedgehog
keep	=	the main tower within a castle or fortress
light cavalry	=	lightly armed and armoured men mounted on horses
longbow	=	a large and powerful weapon that, in the right hands, could fire arrows 240 feet (70 metres) or more

puppet king	=	a ruler who appears to be independent, but is actually controlled by someone else
rearguard	=	troops that guard the rear of an army, especially in retreat
relieve	=	to bring help
sack	=	to plunder and destroy
schiltron	=	a battle formation consisting of circles of soldiers holding long spears pointing outwards in every direction
siege	=	a military operation that involves surrounding a building or place and cutting off supplies and lines of communication
skirmish	=	a brief and often minor fight
standard	=	the flag of a person, place or nation
strategic	=	being in an important place
strong-point	=	a fortified position
terrain	=	ground

QUESTIONS & THINGS TO DO

- What is guerrilla warfare? Can you think of any other fighters who have used this strategy?
- What is a strong-point? Draw a picture of one.
- What sort of weapons were used on the battlefield? Why not draw pictures of them?
- Did you know that each piece of armour has a special name? Draw a picture of a knight dressed in armour and name each piece.
- Draw a picture of Stirling Castle and label each part of it.
- What went wrong for the Scots at the Battle of Falkirk?
- Draw a picture of a schiltron. Can you find out if any other nations used similar battle formations?
- Make a model of the spider that inspired Robert Bruce, or draw a picture of it in the cave where the king was sheltering.

CHAPTER 3

Victory at Bannockburn

The main body of the defenders of Stirling Castle joined their sentries on the battlements early on 23 June 1314. In the gloom they could make out little amid the trees and bogs.

Then they saw what appeared to be several hundred knights riding along the edge of the carse, as if they were trying to get between the Scots army and the castle.

King Edward had ordered them to take up a position where they could harass the Scots once he had carried out his plan to dislodge them with a mammoth frontal assault.

Meanwhile, the advance party of the English cavalry, foot soldiers and archers, led by the Earl of Hereford and the Earl of Gloucester, moved slowly towards the Scots. Bruce, unarmoured and mounted on a light pony, inspected his forward troops, keeping a wary eye on the enemy. While doing so, he accidentally strayed too far from his own lines.

One of the English knights, Sir Henry de Bohun, recognised the Scottish king by the coronet he was wearing on his helmet and decided to charge towards him. Bruce's commanders watched helplessly. They were too far away to go to his aid. If he were killed, all would be lost. Bruce waited calmly until de Bohun's lance point was almost at his chest, then quickly wheeled his pony away. As he did so, he dodged the lance and split de Bohun's helmet and skull with his light battle-axe. A great cheer went up from the Scottish troops.

On being reproved by his commanders for risking his life so near to the fighting, the king merely remarked: 'Alas, I have broken my good battle-axe.'

○ ○ ○

The elated Scottish troops then advanced towards the English vanguard, who charged towards the advancing Scots.

English horses whinnied and reared as they stepped on the pointed calthrops in the pits. Many other mounts were deliberately lanced or hacked by the Scots troops to bring down their heavily armoured riders.

Dust rose in great grey clouds. When it cleared, the defenders of Stirling Castle saw the large English army falling back.

The Scots under the tight control of King Robert, held their positions in the wood of the New Park and were greatly heartened by their initial success.

HASTY SIR HENRY

Generations of Scottish children have chanted an old jingle about Sir Henry de Bohun's hasty charge against King Robert.

> Bruce and de Bohun
> Fought for the croon*
> Bruce took his battle-axe
> And knocked de Bohun doon!

*croon = crown

As you can tell from the verse, Bohun was pronounced 'boon', which rhymed nicely with two other Scottish pronunciations.

Meanwhile an English force was making its way along the edge of the carse, led by Sir Robert Clifford. They had not been seen by Moray's division, whose duty it was to guard that side. Bruce sent messengers with a reprimand, warning him: 'A rose has fallen from your chaplet.'

The stung Moray hurried his schiltrons down to the low ground. The Scots' careful training began to prove itself as they moved quickly in disciplined bodies, spears at the ready.

The English knights then charged the oncoming Scots, who formed a resolute 'hedgehog', and a desperate fight took place.

Knights flung maces and axes into the Scots ring, trying to force an opening so that they could use the weight of their horses, but the spearmen held firm.

Black Douglas became anxious about his hard-pressed comrades, but the king told him to hold his own position and not to go to Moray's aid.

Then Moray's men got their second wind. As the English knights withdrew slightly, the Scots quickly broke 'hedgehog', got into their attack formation and moved forward with their long spears, ready to strike.

○ ○ ○

The castle defenders, trying to make sense of the affray, suddenly saw the English force break up. One half galloped back to the main body of men, the other half headed for the castle. The gates were quickly opened and the English cavalry clattered in. Many of the horses had spear wounds, and some carried wounded men slumped over them or grimly clinging to the reins.

They joined the defenders of the castle they had so eagerly hoped to relieve.

The Scots, on the other hand, were pleased with themselves. They were proud of their success in these probing skirmishes. They had shown that their foot soldiers could beat off an attack by charging knights. Also, they had demonstrated that their often-practised drills were effective in all-out war.

Their king had slain young de Bohun, and the Scots had killed Clifford, one of the commanders of the English cavalry force.

They had dislodged and scattered the body of knights that King Edward had sent to move strategically behind them. This was key, as those knights would have been ready to strike when the moment was right.

They had also blocked the advance of the English army and sent it reeling back.

The opening phases of the battle had gone the Scots' way. It was clear that Bruce's success in single combat with de Bohun had also been a great morale booster.

o o o

King Edward called an urgent council of war in his tent. His angry commandeers pointed out that the tactic of trying to dislodge the Scots from the New Park trees and scrub was hugely difficult because the position was such a strong one. They could not easily work around to the right in an outflanking movement because of the nature of the terrain.

Added to that, the English solders were tired because of their long, forced marches to get to Stirling by the pledged date.
In the middle of all the heated talking and debate, the flaps of the tent parted and a man in a dark cloak entered. It was Sir Philip Mowbray, the commander of the castle. He had sneaked out,

evaded the Scots sentries, and now insisted to King Edward that the castle was technically relieved. After all, half the English force had retreated inside its walls.

But King Edward, angered by the day's reverses, wanted genuine victory. He also needed larger supplies of drinking water for his huge numbers of men and horses, so he decided to move nearer to Stirling.

He planned to cross the Bannockburn and move towards the River Forth, and relieve the castle the next day.

King Edward was sure that Robert Bruce, with his much smaller army, would not leave his prepared positions and attack him.

But Bruce was a superb tactician, and knew his ground. He was fully aware that the carse was low-lying and rough, cut through by the Bannockburn and the Pelstream, and by ditches and pools.

At that time the banks of these burns were steep, and the bottom soft and muddy. There were many bogs, and part of the Bannockburn was tidal where it joined the Forth.

Kind Edward decided to move into this rough territory to get to drier ground. It took a long time to transfer such large numbers of men, and reports say that the wagons could not be moved, so the weary troops ended up with no food. Nevertheless, the men got there and camped for the night.

The English soldiers slept badly, and there were false alarms because the sentries were edgy about the possibility of a Scottish night attack.

○ ○ ○

Bruce had considered breaking off the battle, taking his men into the hills of the west and continuing his guerrilla warfare strategy from there.

But he got valuable information from a Scottish knight Alexander Seton, who had been in King Edward's army and deserted. The knight told Bruce that English morale was low and that their position in the carse was uncomfortable and disorganised.

In addition to this information, Bruce knew that the rough nature of the ground would hamper the cavalry. It would be difficult for the English army to manoeuvre, and this would greatly reduce its superiority in numbers.

He decided to attack them across the carse.

Edward Bruce's division was placed on the right, and Moray and Douglas's divisions slightly back on the left. His own division would be the reserve.

The small folk were moved to the edge of the escarpment as a further reserve. Some think this was done just to keep them out of the way. With such limited ground for movement, an ill-disciplined mob could be a major hindrance.

The few Scottish horsemen were kept well hidden.

It was sunny on 24 June. The castle defenders, still keeping their anxious vigil, had a clear view of the Scots. They saw them moving down from their strong positions on to the flat ground.

It was St John's Day, and the Scottish army attended Mass said by their chaplains. As they knelt in prayer, almost within bow shot of the English army, King Edward is said to have exclaimed: 'They kneel for mercy!' But an English knight replied: 'Yes, sire, but not from you – they mean to attack.'

Quickly, King Edward ordered his knights to saddle. His bowmen drove off the few Scottish archers who were out in front of their advancing spearmen.

The Earl of Gloucester commanded the vanguard of the main English body. He ordered a charge. Edward Bruce's men skilfully formed a hedgehog, and the charge perished in a welter of whinnying horses, broken spears, and the cries of wounded and dying men. Gloucester himself was killed by the Scots spearmen, and the charge was halted.

Moray's division then came storming up on the left and crashed into the English vanguard. It broke and fell back on the main body of men.

o o o

The armies now clanged together in a scrum of hacking, swearing, shouting men. The archers on both sides could not fire for fear of hitting their own comrades.

Douglas's men too pushed forward in formation. Eventually, all three Scottish divisions were engaged in hectic hand-to-hand combat.

The Scots were inferior in numbers, but the narrowness of the front prevented the English army from widening out. The water obstacles, the broken ground and the steady pressure from the front began to cause chaos. Orders were not passed. Men became confused. Those at the front were fiercely engaged. Those behind, pressed together in a tight space, could not reach their enemy or manoeuvre.

The Scottish spearmen kept up the pressure. Their experience and training paid off. As they pressed home their attack, their long spears caused havoc.

But the English army contained many brave and skilled soldiers. A body of archers managed to get onto the Scots' left flank. Soon a hail of arrows began to open up gaps in the Scottish ranks.

For a while it looked as if the failures at the Battle of Falkirk would happen all over again. But Bruce sent an urgent message to Robert Keith, leader of the cavalry, to charge.

The small Scottish cavalry had been anxiously watching the fighting. Now, given their chance, they charged towards the archers. They scattered them and drove them from the field.

A dangerous moment had passed, and the Scots attack regained its momentum.

Bruce now turned to the Macdonalds and the men of the Western Isles in his own and strongest division. To their chief, Angus Og, he gave orders to attack and said: 'My hope is constant in thee!'

○ ○ ○

'On them, on them, they fail, they fail!' shouted the Scots.

Bruce's timing was just right. His division charged into the enemy, and the English lines began to give ground under the renewed pressure.

The Scots scented victory.

The lines of spearmen began to press the English army back on those behind, who could not help them because of the narrow front. Also, the archers at the rear of the English army were out of effective range. They could not be called on in any meaningful way.

Then came an incident that has now passed into legend and stirs pride to this day.

The small folk – the farmers, peasants, fishermen, labourers, herders and huntsmen – with improvised weapons and no discipline, were growing impatient. They had been held in reserve on the escarpment, but they could no longer stand being spectators.

They poured over the edge and pelted towards the fighting armies.

At the sight of what they took to be further Scottish reserves, the main mass of the English army gave way.

A disorganised retreat and near-massacre began.

○ ○ ○

King Edward was persuaded that the day was lost, and retreated to Stirling Castle. However, his bodyguard, Sir Giles d'Argentan, one of his bravest knights, could not stomach retreat and said: 'I am not accustomed to flee, nor am I going to begin now.'

He returned to the battle, charged into the cheering on-coming Scots and was killed.

The main mass of the English army broke towards the Forth. Many perished in the steep gorge of the Bannockburn. Others drowned in the pools and marshes and mud. In places men walked to safety on a grisly bridge formed of dead horses and corpses.

○ ○ ○

The English supply train was captured – a truly amazing haul. At today's prices it would be worth in the region of £7 million.

English casualties were colossal. Nearly all the archers and foot soldiers were killed or captured. Many nobles and knights were also killed, but some were taken prisoner or held to ransom.

Dead bodies could be seen for miles.

Of course, the Scots had suffered as well, particularly in the early fighting. But for them it was an overwhelming victory.

○ ○ ○

At the castle the demoralised garrison again opened the gates to let in a large contingent of fleeing English horsemen.

Sir Philip Mowbray refused to permit King Edward to enter as he felt honour bound to surrender the castle to the Scots.

The king instead escaped to Dunbar. A small boat took him to Berwick and England. There, as the song says, he had 'to think again' (see page 67).

The next day the victorious Scots re-mustered at the castle, and the garrison surrendered.

Edward Bruce's rash promise had turned out successfully. Stirling Castle – the main strategic fortress of Scotland and the focal point of the battle – was once again in the hands of the Scots. It was a major victory in their quest for independence.

THE SMALL FOLK

The part played by the untrained force of Scotsmen, the so-called small folk, in the Battle of Bannockburn was important. When the English troops saw about 2,000 fresh fighters rushing towards them, they panicked. Although the small folk entered the battle late, they may well have been a deciding factor in the English troops' defeat.

It is believed that Gillies Hill (west of Stirling and south of the village of Cambusbarron) is the point from which the small folk descended onto the field of Bannockburn.

WORD LIST

affray	=	a noisy fight
chaplet	=	a circle of flowers worn on the head; it was also the code word that would be used to let Moray know if English troops had got past his schiltrons
demoralised	=	disheartened or downcast
elated	=	very happy and proud
front	=	the area in which opposing armies come face to face
mace	=	a heavy stick with a spiked metal head
morale	=	mental attitude; level of confidence
muster	=	to assemble or gather together
reprimand / reprove	=	to scold or tell off
resolute	=	determined to do something

QUESTIONS & THINGS TO DO

- Design a banner for King Robert Bruce.
- Use modelling clay to make a knight in armour or a Scottish spearman.
- Draw or make a model of King Robert's crown.
- How do you think King Edward felt when Sir Philip Mowbray just walked into his council of war and said the Scots had more or less won? Draw a picture of how the king and his knights might have looked.
- The small folk had only makeshift weapons. What do you think these might have been? Draw a picture of them.
- Look at a map of Stirling (go to www.streetmap.co.uk) and see how many streets you can find that have names linked to the battle.

CHAPTER 4

After the Battle

AFTER THE BATTLE

What happened after the battle? King Edward was almost captured by the Scots, but was shielded by his own knights. He and his bodyguards rode to the gate of Stirling Castle and claimed admission. Governor Mowbray said this would be dishonourable. The Scots had won, so the castle would have to be surrendered to them. King Edward therefore had to turn his horse and head for Linlithgow, where the English had a base for horses and equipment. Once there, he got fresh steeds and retreated to Dunbar Castle, where the Earl of March gave him shelter.

Some historians claim that Edward made a vow to God. He promised that if he escaped, he would establish a house for the religious order called the Poor Carmelites, and dedicate it to Mary, the Mother of God. In fact, he did escape. He obtained a small boat and reached Berwick upon Tweed, just over the border from Scotland. From there he travelled further into England and safety. He kept his word and established the religious house, which eventually evolved into Oriel College at Oxford University.

He never returned to Scotland.

○ ○ ○

King Robert Bruce's position as Scottish king was greatly strengthened by the victory at Bannockburn. It also allowed him to negotiate the return of many high-profile Scottish prisoners. These included his wife and daughter, Queen Elizabeth and Princess Marjorie, who had been held in England. They were exchanged for some prominent English prisoners, including the Earl of Hereford.

MASSACRE AT THE ABBEY

As the Battle of Bannockburn entered its final stages, the retreating English soldiers attacked Bruce's supply depot at Cambuskenneth Abbey, not far from the castle. This was an important site because it held Bruce's horses and supply wagons. It also acted as a hospital for his wounded men, and for local people who been injured even though they had taken no part in the fighting.

When the English attacked the depot, they were angry and vengeful and they did a very wicked thing. They killed all the wounded. This was widely regarded as a dastardly act.

Appeal for independence

Although Bannockburn was a resounding victory for the Scots, English monarchs continued to make a claim for Scotland. They even tried to get support from important people overseas.

In medieval times, England was a Catholic country. King Edward therefore tried to enlist support from Pope John XXII. He was head of the Roman Catholic Church at that time. Previous popes had endorsed Scottish independence, but John XXII accepted the English king's claim to Scotland. In 1319 he even summoned four Scottish bishops to answer accusations of rebellion. This course of events made King Robert Bruce and his followers very angry. It led to one of the most heart-stirring documents in European history.

The Declaration of Arbroath, sometimes called the Declaration of Independence, was a letter sent to Pope John XXII on behalf of the people of Scotland.

Dated 3 April 1320, it was written in Latin at the Abbey of Arbroath by its abbot, Bernard of Linton. He also happened to be Chancellor of Scotland, so he was an important man. For extra effect, it was sealed by eight earls and thirty-one barons.

The document, which exists to this day in government archives, emphasises Scotland's ancient roots and defends Robert Bruce's actions. It gives a blunt warning that the Scottish people will not tolerate the cause for independence being diluted or substituted. The oft-quoted words state:

... we have been set free by our most tireless prince, King and lord, the lord Robert .... Yet if he should give up what he has begun, seeking to make us or our kingdom subject to the King of England or the English, we should exert ourselves at once to drive him out as our enemy ... and make some other man who was well able to defend us our King.

As long as but a hundred of us remain alive, never will we on any conditions be brought under English rule. It is in truth not for glory, nor riches, nor honours, that we are fighting, but for freedom – for that alone, which no honest man gives up but with life itself.

The Battle of Bannockburn, however, was not the end of the war for independence. The English king had escaped, but his reputation was tarnished.

The Scots continued to carry out raids into the north of England, and by 1318 Berwick was the only Scottish town still held by the English. It was eventually taken back by Sir James Douglas.

In a series of bruising encounters, Edward II tried to recover Berwick, but failed. He was deposed in 1327 and his wife, Queen Isabella, took power on behalf of her young son Edward III.

Wearied of war with Scotland, the English entered into the famous 1328 Treaty of Edinburgh-Northhampton, and finally renounced all claims to sovereignty over Scotland.

WORD LIST

dastardly	=	cowardly; despicable
dilute	=	to make weaker or less forceful
endorse	=	to approve
seal	=	a design, often on a ring, that is pressed into wax melted onto a document; in the past a seal was regarded as proof that the document was genuine

QUESTIONS & THINGS TO DO

- Try to find out about the Poor Carmelite order. What sort of life did they lead, and why do you think King Edward wanted to help them in particular?
- The Declaration of Arbroath is kept in the National Archives of Scotland (www.nas.gov.uk). Take a look at the document online, then read the modern English translation.
- Look at the seals on the document. Why not design one for yourself?

CHAPTER 5

Remembering Bannockburn

At the time the Battle of Bannockburn was fought, the countryside was quite empty. It had just a few small villages, and the people who lived there scratched out a very poor existence. Nonetheless, it was their home, and they wanted it to be governed by Scottish leaders.

The following poem was written after the battle and expresses how the Scots felt to have won their liberty. Underneath the verse in Scottish dialect is a translation into modern English.

Freedom

JOHN BARBOUR (c.1330–95)

A! fredome is a noble thing!
Fredome mayes man to haiff liking;
Fredome all solace to man giffis:
He levys at ess that freely levys!

Freedom is a noble thing!
Great happiness does freedom bring;
All solace to a man it gives;
He lives at ease that freely lives!

Robert Burns, Scotland's national bard and internationally acclaimed poet, visited the battle site at Bannockburn on 26 August 1787. Afterwards he penned one of Scotland's best-known songs. To many people it has the status of an anthem and is known as 'Scots Wha Hae' (which means 'Scots who have'). It can be played to a number of tunes, including the old air 'Hey Tutti Taitie'.

Scots Wha Hae

Scots, wha hae wi Wallace bled,
Scots, wham Bruce has aften led,
Welcome to your gory bed,
    Or to victorie!

Now's the day, and now's the hour:
See the front o battle lour,
See approach proud Edward's power –
    Chains and slaverie!

Wha will be a traitor knave?
Wha can fill a coward's grave?
Wha sae base as be a slave?
    Let him turn, an flee!

Wha for Scotland's King and Law
Freedom's sword will strongly draw,
Freeman stand, or Freeman fa',
    Let him follow me!

By Oppression's woes and pains,
By your sons in servile chains,
We will drain your dearest veins
    But they shall be free!

Lay the proud usurpers low!
Tyrants fall in every foe!
Liberty's in every blow! –
    Let us do, or die!

There are many other old songs about Scottish independence, including 'The Thistle o' Scotland'. In modern times another song has emerged that pays tribute to what happened at Bannockburn. Called 'O Flower of Scotland', it was written by Roy Williamson of the Corries folk group:

> O Flower of Scotland,
> When will we see your like again
> That fought and died for
> Your wee bit hill and glen.
> And stood against him,
> Proud Edward's army,
> And sent him homeward
> To think again.

This popular song has become the country's unofficial national anthem. It has also been adopted as the official anthem of Scotland's football and rugby teams.

Bannockburn today

There has been controversy over the centuries about the ground where the Battle of Bannockburn was actually fought. However, there has always been a local belief that Bruce's command post was sited in the area known as the Borestone. This is named after a prominent stone in which a hole was bored for holding the king's standard.

In 1932 this site came under the control of the National Trust for Scotland. Since then it has become a popular destination for visitors. In fact, so many people came to visit that an iron grille had to be placed over the Borestone to prevent visitors digging out bits of it as souvenirs.

A huge flagpole marks the battlefield site. This is close to the modern visitor centre.

A magnificent equestrian statue of King Robert Bruce, sculpted by Pilkington Jackson, was erected in 1964. It was formally dedicated to the Scottish king by Queen Elizabeth.

WORD LIST

anthem	=	a song that expresses loyalty to a person, place or organisation
controversy	=	argument or debate
dialect	=	a form of language spoken in a particular area or by a particular group of people; Scots is a dialect of English
equestrian	=	on horseback
freeman	=	a person who is not a slave or a serf (a serf was a labourer bound to work for a lord)
lour	=	to appear menacing
servile	=	like a slave
usurper	=	a person who takes something without authorisation

QUESTIONS & THINGS TO DO

- Visit the battlefield site and centre.
- How do you think Robert Bruce would feel about having a statue dedicated to him?
- Why not try to write your own poem or song about Bannockburn? You could write it from the point of view of a commander, spearman or one of the small folk.

ALSO BY RENNIE McOWAN

The Dumyat Series

Follow the thrilling adventures of Gavin and his friends Michael, Clare and Mot in four exciting books. The first, *Light on Dumyat*, involves robbers; the second, *The White Stag Adventure*, has mysterious incidents at a ruined castle; in the third, *The Day the Mountain Moved*, they go back in time and meet figures from Scottish Celtic mythology; and in the fourth, *Jewels on the Move*, they save some very valuable precious stones. Educational and very exciting, *The Dumyat Series* is widely used in Scottish schools.

Robert Burns for Beginners

Young people studying the work of Robert Burns find few specially produced volumes to work from, so this book fills an important gap. It includes an introduction to the life of Burns, samples of his poetry and songs, advice and instructions on how to organise a Burns Supper, plus project suggestions for class and individual participation.

St Andrew for Beginners

The story of how Andrew went from being a simple fisherman in Galilee to becoming one of the first Christians and eventually patron saint of Scotland makes fascinating reading. *St Andrew for Beginners* outlines what is known about the life and times of Andrew, contains a short history of the Celtic Church, and takes a brief look at the other patron saints of the British Isles. The book also includes suggestions for individual and group projects.

All titles available from Rowan Tree Publishing, Lochbank House, Castle Douglas DG7 1TH   www.rowantreepublishing.co.uk